# YOUR KNOWLEDGE HAS VALUE

**Bibliographic information published by the German National Library:**

The German National Library lists this publication in the National Bibliography;
detailed bibliographic data are available on the Internet at http://dnb.dnb.de .

**Imprint:**

Copyright © 2013 GRIN Verlag, Open Publishing GmbH
Print and binding: Books on Demand GmbH, Norderstedt Germany
ISBN: 9783656438083

**This book at GRIN:**

http://www.grin.com/en/e-book/214854/migrants-strangers-and-the-church-in-
southern-africa-a-biblical-perspective

**Thorsten Prill**

**NETS Theological Research Papers**

Band 2

# Migrants, Strangers and the Church in Southern Africa. A Biblical Perspective

**NETS Theological Research Papers - Volume Two**

GRIN Publishing

**GRIN - Your knowledge has value**

Since its foundation in 1998, GRIN has specialized in publishing academic texts by students, college teachers and other academics as e-book and printed book. The website www.grin.com is an ideal platform for presenting term papers, final papers, scientific essays, dissertations and specialist books.

# Migrants, Strangers and the Church in Southern Africa:
# A Biblical Perspective

## NETS Theological Research Papers
## Volume Two

Thorsten Prill

Senior Lecturer

Namibia Evangelical Theological Seminary

# Contents

# Glossary

**Asylum**
Protection granted by a country to a person who has left his or her own country as a political refugee.

**Ethnicity**
State of belonging to a social group which has a common cultural or national tradition.

**Ethnocentrism**
The evaluation of other cultures or nations according to preconditions which originate in the customs, values and norms of one's own culture or nation.

**Migrant**
A person who moves from one place to another (often crossing national borders) in order to find work or better living conditions.

**Racism**
Prejudice and discrimination directed against someone who belongs to a different race which is based on the conviction that one's own race is superior.

**Refugee**
A forced migrant, i.e. a person who has been forced to leave his or her own country in order to escape persecution, war or natural disaster.

**Tribalism**
Negative behaviour and attitudes that derive from strong loyalty to one's own tribe or social group.

**Xenophobia**
A strong fear or dislike of people from other countries or nations.

# Ethnocentrism and xenophobia in southern Africa

In 2008 many people in Africa and elsewhere were shocked when they saw on their televisions how Zimbabwean, Mozambican and Malawian immigrants were attacked, robbed and beaten up in South African townships. This eruption of xenophobic violence against millions of fellow southern Africans was unheard of. The following witness report was published in an article by BBC correspondent Caroline Hawley (2008):

> I ran away from the situation in Zimbabwe to try to support my family...But it's better to starve at home than to die here. At least, if I'm back in Zimbabwe, my parents can bury me and see my grave....They forced their way into my home with weapons, hammers and bricks. And they took everything I've got. The only things I have left are the clothes that I'm wearing. I don't even know how I'll get home.

The riots of 2008 'left 62 people dead and about 150,000 displaced, primarily foreign nationals and members of South Africa's ethnic minorities' (Segatti 2011:10). These attacks in South African townships were surely an extreme expression of ethnic, tribal and national hatred and were not unrelated events. Racism, tribalism, ethnocentrism and selfish national interests are still widespread not only in South Africa but also in other African countries (:11). For example, the Namibian scholar Gerhard Tötemeyer (2010:180) argues that racism, tribalism and ethnocentrism have not been overcome in his home country that gained independence from South Africa in 1990 ending the discriminating phase of Apartheid. Referring to the prophetic mission of the church he strongly believes that it is the church which has a crucial role to play to bring about reconciliation and justice in the Namibian society. He writes:

> In the Namibian context it includes bridging existing barriers and divisions between Blacks and Whites, between Blacks and Blacks, between Whites and Whites, between ethnicities, between tribes, between classes and between victims and perpetrators of injustice. It is unfortunate that the concept 'race' still figures in comparisons and arguments instead of referring to one race, the human race. The process of deracination is still incomplete.

While the Church is visibly present in southern African societies it seems that the biblical teaching on migrants, strangers and ethnic minorities has had little impact so far. Tribalism and xenophobia can be found inside and outside southern African church walls. While restrictive immigration policies are common (cf. Klotz 2000:831), national immigration departments can be very selective and biased when it comes to granting fellow southern Africans work or study permits. In the name of nation interests highly qualified workers from neighbouring countries are expelled though there is a need for their services. Renu Modi (2003:1760) writes about the situation in South Africa:

> The immigration policy the world over is restrictive and does not allow un-restricted access across its borders. States do have a sovereign right to protect their own citizen's interests by regulating its borders. The South African policy therefore is no different. What differentiates the South African policy is a total lack of commitment to minimum human rights standards agreed upon by the international community, to which South Africa is a signatory.

According to Segatti (2011:9) the situation is not much different in other southern African countries. Thus, she states that 'Southern Africa's national policies and regional initiatives remain marooned in an approach rigidly based on border control and national sovereignty'. The responses to increased levels of migrations by southern Africa governments can be described as 'defensive and noncommittal' (:9). One of the reasons for such an attitude is the perception of immigrants as a threat to the economic and social well-being of the country and its population (Modi 2003:1760-1761). Countries like South Africa, Botswana and Namibia 'have achieved levels of political stability and economic growth that the ruling parties...wish to sustain' (Segatti 2011:11).

Unfortunately, the situation within the African Church is often not much better. Many denominations and local churches are organised along ethnic/tribal lines. One of the main historical reasons for this is the fact that western missionaries tended to work in specific regions and focused on particular language groups (Pohor 2006:316). Where churches today embrace more than one ethnicity these groups often exist more or less separately from each other. Truly multicultural churches and denominations are still the exception. And while most church leaders would agree that the Church of Christ is a global body there are some among them who try hard to remove their fellow leaders just because they do not share the same nationality or ethnic/tribal background. Evans Chama (2010), writing from a Roman Catholic perspective, comments:

> In many African countries tribalism has determined who becomes president and holds important positions. Unfortunately, this has often also been an issue in both the appointment and reception of a new bishop. A person from a different tribe, especially when that tribe is a minority, is seen as an intruder coming to take away power. When we act like this way, not only do we abuse the positive development of having a local person as a shepherd, but also lose absolutely the sense of Church. That's why, without making reference to any particular case, some people would receive it as an insult to have a foreign missionary appointed as their bishop.

Surely there is a huge gap between the testimony of the Bible and everyday southern African reality. However, Punt (2009:269) clearly goes too far when he identifies 'stereotyping and vilifying language' in the Bible and a naïve reading of the Bible 'based on claims about verbal inspiration and unhistorical assumption' as the reasons for recent 'racist practices and xenophobic attacks' in South Africa. On the contrary, the biblical teaching rejects racism and promotes acceptance beyond ethnic and social boundaries. The purpose of this article is to give an overview of what the Scriptures have to say about these issues and to encourage Christians to live accordingly and to promote the biblical view in their local communities and beyond.

# Migrants in the Bible

In his book *Asylum and Immigration – A Christian Perspective on a Polarised Debate* Nick Spencer (2004:85) rightly points out that the concept of asylum cannot be found in the Scriptures. But this does not mean that both the Old and the New Testament have nothing to say about migration and migrants. Apart from the Book of Daniel and Psalms 78 and 137, wisdom literature and psalms are silent on the issue of migration. However, the theme of forced migration is very prominent in the Pentateuch and the history books. In the New Testament the theme of wandering and homelessness plays an important role.

## Abraham and his family

One of the most prominent stories of migration in the Old Testament is the story of Abraham and his family. The book of Genesis tells us about their journey of migration. In chapter 12 we are informed that Abram, originally from Ur in Mesopotamia, is called by God to leave Haran and to go to Canaan. Cotter (2003:90) writes about Abram's call:

> Abram is commanded to leave three things: country, kindred, and his father's home. Thus, he is to leave behind the past, everything and everyone familiar to him, all the previous supports and influences he has known, and to depend on God alone.

However, God's command to go to an unknown country is accompanied by a promise. The significance of this promise goes far beyond Abraham and his family: God will make him a great nation through which all families on the earth will be blessed (Westermann 1987:98). Walter Brueggemann (1982:121) depicts Abraham's migration as a metaphor of a journey that characterizes the life of faith. Abraham's journey, he argues, must not only be understood as a physical movement (:121). It stands for the life of faith. It is the life of faith which keeps Abraham and his descendants in pursuit of the land that God has promised them (:122). This metaphor of a journey is not only radically different from our modern western ideologies which long for 'settlement, security and placement', it also reflects something of God's character (:122). Brueggemann writes: 'Thus Yahweh is understood not as a God who settles and dwells, but as a God who sojourns and moves about' (:122).

Chapters 12:10-20 explain that severe famine was the reason for Abram not immediately settling in Canaan, and the cause of his flight to Egypt. Here, he asks his wife Sarai to pretend to be his sister. This is, as Turner (2000:65-66) writes, a lie. He continues: 'Not only is it intrinsically improbable, but 11.29 which told us of Abram's marriage also told us that his brother Nahor married his niece' (:66). Turner concludes that any blood relationship between Abram and Sarai would certainly have been mentioned too (:66). According to Gibson (1990:34) it was simple cowardice of Abram that caused him to ask his wife to pose as his sister. Amos (2004:79) considers his behaviour as pure selfishness. She writes:

> Abram's next actions don't cover him with glory either. He is selfishly far more concerned with his own safety (*they will kill me*) than with protecting his wife Sarai or preserving her dignity. Abram acknowledges that her life would never have been in danger: *they will let you live*. Sarai is treated merely as a chattel to be traded for Abram's own advantage.

Gibson's and Amos' judgement appears harsh but there were good reasons for Abram's fear. Firstly, as an alien in Egypt he was powerless and especially vulnerable as a Hebrew (Hamilton 1990:380). Secondly, it was not unusual for powerful rulers to abduct married women. Both King David and the Mesopotamian king Gilgamesh acted exactly in this way (Janzen 1993:24). Thirdly, Abram's fear that he could be killed but his wife would be spared was quite realistic (Wenham 1987:291). This was exactly the practice of a later King of Egypt (Exod. 1:16).

Lack of rain for extensive periods automatically induced famines in the agrarian societies of the ancient Near East. Old Testament accounts of famine record dramatic rises in the cost of food (2 Kgs. 6:24-25) and cannibalism (Lam. 2:20). Sometimes famines even led to the breakdown of whole societies and migration to other countries. In addition to Abram the Old Testament cites the examples of Isaac who leaves his home country for Gerar (Gen. 26:7) and Joseph's family who seek refuge in the Egyptian district of Goshen (Gen. 47:4-6) (Hudiburg 2000:455-456). Westermann (1987:103) speaks of famines as 'one of the fundamental experiences of human misery'.

Finally, the story of Abraham's migration needs to be seen in the light of God's mission to bring salvation to the ends of the earth: The migrant Abraham 'will become the means of blessing for all humankind' (Köstenberger & O'Brien 2001:30). Girgis (2011:70) notes:

> The biblical writer highlights Abraham's and Sarah's ministry and life as a story of sojourners for good reason: to get our attention to God's purpose towards the nations as we "go to all nations" (Matt. 28), to "gather all nations and tongues" (Is. 66:18), to "bless the nations" (Gen. 12) and to bring different people together to form God's reign "on earth as it is in heaven". To bring people in, Abraham had to get out, leaving his own country and kindred, and journey to the unknown, becoming a stranger and a sojourner.

## The exodus

The first chapter of the Book of Exodus tells the story of the Israelites' oppression in Egypt. After a long and prosperous period the Israelites are forced into slavery. Two reasons are given by the narrator. Firstly, a new pharaoh comes to power. Ashby (1998:9) speaks of 'a new dynasty as a result of some sort of coup'. Some scholars believe this new ruler to be Rameses II (cf. Clements 1972:11; Coggins 2000:5; Cole 1973:43; Noth 1962:22; Sarna 1991:4). Others think that the new pharaoh was either Rameses II or his predecessor Seti (cf. Davies 1973:40). Meyers (2005), however, argues that the name of this pharaoh was left out deliberately by the author. He notes:

> It is more likely that the pharaoh is intentionally unnamed. The anonymity of key figures in biblical narratives can serve rhetorical purposes. By not having a specific name, the pharaoh who subjugates the Israelites can represent all such oppressors. At the very least, denying him a name may serve to demean him (:34).

With this change of regime the situation for Jacob's descendants has radically changed too. The writer informs us that the new ruler does not know Joseph (Exod. 1:8). In other words, he is not obliged to respect any commitment to a group of foreigners within his territory (Durham 1987:7; Fretheim 1991:27). Secondly, the expansion of the Hebrew population is seen as potentially damaging in two ways: the new regime fears that they could ally themselves with foreign powers and that they could diminish the workforce by leaving the country (Exod. 1:9-10). The bondage pharaoh prescribes for the Israelites is not slavery as such but rather forced labour (Meyers 2005:34). Sarna (1986:21) speaks of a 'state slavery' which imposes 'forced labour upon the male population for long and indefinite terms of service under degrading and brutal conditions'. What the narrative does not explain is how the new Egyptian regime expected the forced labour to impede the increase of the Hebrews (Childs 1974:15). Janzen (1997:19) notes that by enslaving the Israelites, the Egyptians had obtained a cheap labour source for improving their infrastructure. In verse 11 we can read that the Israelites had to build supply cities for the Egyptians. In sum, the oppression of the Israelites appears to be politically and economically motivated. This oppression reaches a new level when the new Egyptian ruler orders the death of every newborn male child (Exod. 1:15-16). Van Seters (1994:23) comments that the term genocide 'seems to deal more directly with the threat of Israel's increased population in Exodus 1'.

The biblical evidence gives clear grounds for the rise of nationalism and racism in Egypt of the 13th century BC. A political climate is created which is ripe for manipulation. The Egyptian king 'plays on the prejudices and fears of his own people to justify his own racist attitudes' (Ashby 1998:10). The story of the exodus presents a classical example of racial conflict. It shows how racial prejudices lead to persecution and oppression, coupled with economic exploitation, and thus to forced migration (:10).

According to Garrett (1990:656), the exodus from Egypt, which is told in chapters 12 to 18, was the 'paradigm of historical renewal' for the early Israelites. For Guiterrez Israel's exodus forms a paradigm for liberation theology (Tombs 2002:128). Guiterrez (2001:154) sees it as a political event. He writes:

> The liberation of Israel is a political action. It is the breaking away from a

9

situation of despoliation and misery and the beginning of the construction of a just and comradely society. It is the suppression of disorder and the creation of a new order.

Guiterrez is undoubtedly right that there is an element of political liberation in the exodus story. However, there is also a strong spiritual aspect (Prill 2005:326). Thus, the starting point of Israel's liberation is that 'God remembered his covenant with Abraham, Isaac, and Jacob' (Exod. 2:24). The basis of this covenant is an act of faith. Genesis 17:7 tells us that God not only established a covenant with Abraham, who believed in the Lord (Gen. 15:6), but also with his descendants. In other words, God entered into a covenant with Abraham's descendants on the basis of his faith, or as Köstenberger & O'Brien (2001:34) put it: 'Israel is not entering a covenant of works, that is conditional or provisional, but is responding to a covenant of grace based on divine promises made earlier with Abraham.' Consequently, the exodus story is a story of 'the God who acts in salvation' (Cole 1985:27). As such it points to 'Christ, our Passover Lamb' (1 Cor. 5:7). It points to the ultimate salvation, the ultimate liberation which Christ achieved through His death on the cross.

## The Babylonian exile

Another Old Testament example of migration is the Babylonian Exile. In this instance it is a foreign power that forces people to leave their home country. The author of 2 Kings gives an account of two deportations of people from Judah to Babylon. The significance of the first deportation was that the people taken to Babylon all belonged to the ruling class, the Jerusalem establishment (Hobbs 1985:352). Thus, the deportees were members of the royal family, officials of the royal court, soldiers, and skilled craftsmen (2 Kgs. 24:16). Only the poorest people remained in Jerusalem (24:14). Robinson (1976:237) identifies the reason for these deportations:

> Nebuchadnezzar did not depopulate the city. He removed those who might assist in a future rebellion, *the officers and fighting men* who would provide the army, and *the craftsmen and smiths* who would make weapons for them to use.

After Zedekiah's rebellion against Nebuchadnezzar a second deportation took place. This time there were three groups of people who were exiled: those who were left in Jerusalem, the deserters and the rest of the population (25:11). Again we are told that only some of the poorest people were allowed to stay. They were left to look after the vineyards and the farmland (25:12).

The fundamental reason for the Babylonian invasion and the deportations lies in Nebuchadnezzar's hunger for power. It was his aim to subdue the Philistine cities and to get control over Judah (Jones 1984:633). Removal of social elites reduced the possibility of future revolt. But there was also an underlying economic agenda in operation. It is striking that the rich, the educated and the qualified people are deported to Babylon, while the poor are left behind in Judah. Only those are taken into exile that are of use for the Babylonian economy in general and the war economy specifically. At the same time the economic basis for the state of Judah is almost completely destroyed. That the Babylonians have a special interest in Israelite human capital is demonstrated in the story of Daniel and the other young Israelites of royal descent. These young men are valued by the Babylonians because of their wisdom and knowledge. They receive further training and function as advisers to the Babylonian King (Dan. 1:3-8).

Psalm 137 reveals something of the feelings of the exiled people of Judah. It shows the sufferings of a people who experienced the destruction of their homeland, who were deported to a foreign country, and who, upon their return, have to live in a ruined city (Weiser 1962:794). The psalm speaks about pain and homesickness. There is the pain of being separated from one's homeland. There is the pain of being cut-off from one's religious centre. The exiled people of Judah find it difficult to practise their religion: 'How could we sing the LORD's song in a foreign land? If I forget you, O Jerusalem, let my right hand wither' (Ps. 137:4-5). Kraus (1989:503) comments:

> The songs of Zion glorify Yahweh. But such Yahweh hymns cannot be sung in a foreign land. Cultic practice is not possible here (cf. 1 Sam 26:19; Hosea 8:3ff.). The land is unclean (cf. Ezek. 4:13). And yet, this explanation in v.4 does not preclude having a service of lamentation in a foreign land (cf. 1 Kings 8:46ff.).

Furthermore, Psalm 137 speaks about wrath and revenge: 'O daughter of Babylon, you devastator! Happy shall they be who pay you back what you have done to us' (:8). According to Schaefer (2001:323), this curse should not be understood literally. It is rather 'an overflow of feeling beautifully captured in a restrained composition'. Other scholars interpret verses 8 and 9 differently. Weiser (1962:797) writes that it is a real outburst of hatred that can be found in these verses while Knight (1983:315) speaks of a cruel prayer and Stuhlmueller (2002:144) of a scandal. Rogerson and McKay (1977:150) argue that one cannot deny the vindictive character of these words. However, they must be seen in the context of the Jewish belief in a just God and in Jerusalem as God's dwelling place. Rogerson and McKay continue: 'The Israelites could not conceive that a nation that had lifted up its hand to destroy God's sanctuary would escape punishment' (:150). Broyles (1999:480) points out 'that Psalm 137 is in the mouth of powerless victims, not powerful executioners' while Berlin (2005:69) argues that these verses not only contain thoughts of retaliation but are a kind of retaliation themselves. Instead of receiving the songs of joy that the captors have asked for they receive a song of doom. Berlin goes on to say that the 'rock' is a synonym of Edom itself. She concludes: 'The gist of verse 9 is that the rock-fortress protecting Edom will be the instrument for Edom's own punishment' (:70). In whatever way one understands these verses, Psalm 137 makes clear that refugees are people with feelings, sometimes with very strong feelings. Those who wish to help them need to empathise with their emotional and spiritual states.

## Ruth and Naomi

In his commentary on Judges and Ruth Victor Matthews (2004:215) writes that '[a] large portion of scholarship on Ruth has centred on legal issues, especially the terms of levirate marriage or obligation'. Thus, Sakenfeld (1999:6) identifies the levirate marriage as one of the central customs underlying the story, while Younger (2002:399-403) considers the levirate marriage and the kinsman-redeemer concept as the central background issues. For Sakenfeld (1999:11) there are two main theological themes: firstly, the joy of community life; and secondly, loyalty in one's personal relationships. Moore (2000:300) however, points to another theme: wandering and restoration.

Two examples of migration can be found in the Book of Ruth. The book begins with an account of Elimelech's migration to Moab, which is economically motivated. Because of a famine in the land of Judah, Elimelech and his family leave their home town of Bethlehem and settle in their neighbouring country (Ruth 1:1-2). Further, chapter one gives an account of a second migration. Having heard about the end of the famine, Elimelech's widow Naomi decides to return to Judah (:6-7), and Ruth, her daughter-in-law insists on going with her: 'Do not press me to leave you or to turn back from following you! Where you go, I will go; where you lodge, I will lodge; your people shall be my people, and your God my God' (1:16). Ruth's decision is not motivated by economic but by personal, cultural, and religious reasons.

Firstly, there is a strong family bond between Ruth and Naomi. Ruth's 'commitment to go with Naomi and to lodge with her incorporates the personal dimension of the companionship and support Ruth offers to her mother-in-law' (Sakenfeld 1999:31). Being confronted with the painful choice between her love for Naomi and the hope of a second marriage in her home country, she decides to stay with her husband's mother (cf. Atkinson 1999:45-46). She is willing to give up the security of a husband in order to help her mother-in-law to find a new security in Bethlehem (Hamlin 1996:19).

Secondly, Ruth, the Moabitess feels a strong affiliation with the people of Israel. With the declaration 'your people shall be my people' Ruth renounces her ethnic origin and adopts the nationality of her mother-in-law (Hubbard 1988:117). Coxon (1989:26) writes that Ruth's confession 'Judaizes' her. Matthews (2004:222) speaks of an 'assimilation ritual': Bethlehem will be Ruth's new social place and that she will have to comply with the social norms of that place. In contrast to Coxon and Matthews, Sakenfeld (1999:32) argues that Ruth's commitment to Israel does not go that far. '[The] story of Ruth', writes Sakenfeld, 'does not claim that she totally assimilates or abandons her cultural identity.' She continues: 'The repeated references to her Moabite ancestry point not only to resistance in Bethlehem, but also to her legitimate claim to participate as a Moabite in the life of the Bethlehem community' (:32).

Thirdly, Ruth not only commits herself to Naomi and the people of Israel, but also to the God of Israel. Like Rahab (Josh. 2: 8-14) and Naaman (2 Kgs. 5:1-

18) Ruth converts to covenantal faith (House 1998:457). Sakenfeld (1999:32) suggests that there is a difference between Ruth's commitment to the people of Israel and the faith of Israel. She writes:

> Ruth's formal commitment to a different religious faith is a still more momentous decision, for in the case of religion…an abandoning of the former faith is expected. In Jewish tradition, Ruth is remembered as the paradigmatic example of conversion. Rabbinic writers interpreted her speech as a declaration of conversion and deduced from her words requirements to be accepted by all converts.

Some commentators have challenged the notion of Ruth's conversion. Moore (2000:322), for example, believes that one cannot say what Ruth means exactly by God. He continues:

> While many translations (including NIV) singularize and capitalize *'elohim* as "God", it is just as likely that Ruth speaks to Naomi as Naomi earlier spoke to her, as one Syro-Palestinian to another, using theological language more at home in the polytheistic world of Mesha, Balaam, and Micah (Judg. 17-18) than in the monotheistic world of the Mishnah or the NT (:322).

While Moore is right that the term *elohim* can be translated both as 'God' or 'Gods' (cf. McLaughlin 2000:401-402), he seems to overlook the fact that Ruth's faith in the God of Israel is confirmed by her actions (cf. Younger 2002:425). Younger (2002:425) summarises the meaning of Ruth's declaration well when he writes: '[T]he essence of the oath is that only death will separate Ruth from Naomi. Her commitment to Naomi transcends even the bonds of racial origin and national religion: Naomi's people and Naomi's God will henceforth be hers.' Ruth's commitment to Naomi goes even beyond life. Hamlin (1996:20) notes: 'Orpha went back to her own people and would be buried with her ancestors, but Ruth's solidarity with Naomi extended even to death and burial by her side, as foremothers of the people of Israel.'

The Book of Ruth is clearly a study in God's providence (Craghan 1982:198). It shows that the God of Israel cares for people who face dangerous situations. He provides by urging others to react to human tragedy. Hubbard (1988:69-70) comments:

> [If] the story presumes divine action at all, it must be through human agents. Thus, while posting a sign of God's presence at the beginning, the author spoke of his subsequent activity with startling indirectness. Far from downplaying God's providence in the story, however, the indirectness only heightens the reader's awareness of it. As a powerful stylistic device, extreme understatement served as effective overstatement to stress forcefully that Yahweh is indeed very much at work.

God's care is a 'care for those in danger of being left on society's margins' (Campbell 1999:663). In the Ruth story this is typified by the two widows, one an Israelite and one a foreigner (:663). Furthermore, the author stresses Ruth's ethnic origin (LaSor, Hubbard & Bush 1982:615). Thus, he identifies Ruth as a Moabitess in several places where her national and cultural origin is actually of no real interest (Ruth 1:2, 2:2, 4:4, 4:10). By doing so, he underlines the fact that God's love and providence are not limited to the people of Israel but go beyond ethnic boundaries. Last but not least, the author stresses that the ethnically mixed marriage of Boaz and Ruth will lead to David into whose line God will send his son, the savior of the world (Eaton 2000:124). In other words, the story of Ruth serves as a 'reminder of God's clear and intentional purpose of establishing a "house of prayer for all people" where there will be "no longer Jew or Greek, slave or free, male or female", as people "come from east and west, north and south and recline at table", the one and same table that manifests "God's kingdom on earth as it is in heaven" (Girgis 2011:71).

## Jesus and his family

The most prominent refugee story of the New Testament can be found in the Gospel of Matthew. In Matt. 2:13-23 the cause of migration is cited: after having been warned by an angel, Joseph takes Mary and Jesus and together they flee to Egypt in order to escape from King Herod who wants to kill their newborn child. Davies (1993:38), and others, argue that it is unlikely that this flight really happened. Schweizer (1976:44) points out that the Jewish historian Josephus, who accurately writes about the cruelties of Herod, does not mention the slaughter of infants. Beare (1981:82) claims that Matthew introduces the story only so that he can quote from Hosea 11:1. 'There is no reason to believe', writes Beare, 'that is has any historical basis.' Luz (1989:146) comments on the historicity of the periscope as follows:

> It is inexplicable why the devious fox Herod would wait so long until a politically mass murder was feasible. Our narrative is connected with the almost certainly unhistorical Bethlehem tradition and has no analogy at all in Luke. Only one point must be taken seriously: One has to ask whether there is perhaps a kernel of truth behind the tradition of Jesus' stay in Egypt: Judaism is aware of this tradition, and that in a form, it seems to me, in its oldest shape excludes dependence on Matthew.

Other scholars hold that the story is quite plausible. Albright and Mann (1971:17) argue that if one accepts the historicity of the birth narrative in the Gospel of Luke, then even a rumour of the events described in Luke 2:1-19 would certainly have caused a violent tyrannical reaction like that of Herod. Hagner's thesis supports this view when he writes: 'The story is consistent with what we know of Herod and reflects the way he would have responded to the announcement of the magi' (Hagner 1993:35). The fact that there are no references to the killing of infants in other historical sources is not surprising, since the number of children slaughtered by Herod was probably relatively small (:35). Also, in biblical times Egypt was not only the place of Israel's enslavement but also a traditional place of refuge for Jewish people (Senior 1998:47; Davies & Allison 2000:259). Blomberg (1992:66) even speaks of Egypt as 'a natural haven for first-century Jews', while Girgis (2011:72) puts it is this way:

> While Egypt's image as the land of bondage and slavery seems to be dominant among Western Christians, in many places the scriptures draw a quite different image of Egypt. Egypt was mentioned more than 587 times in the Bible, and in the majority of these places, Egypt is viewed as a land of refuge where people seek food, security and protection. Abraham, Joseph, Jacob, Moses, the twelve tribes of Israel and, last but not least, the holy family itself, all went to Egypt as refugees escaping from famine and persecution.

There are many more examples. 1 Kings 12:40 records the fact that Jeroboam, the son of Nebat, fled to Egypt because King Solomon tried to kill him. The cause of conflict was Jeroboam's rebellion against the king (1 Kgs. 11). Jeremiah 41:16-18 cites a further example: a group of soldiers, women and children under the leadership of Johanan, son of Kareah, went to Egypt to escape Babylonian captivity.

The reason for the flight to Egypt, as Matthew presents it, is the fear of persecution. Herod the Great's persecution is politically motivated. The title 'king of the Jews', that is used by the magi in chapter 2, verse 2, has a political connotation (Hagner 1993:27). King Herod was a cruel and vindictive ruler, who was well versed in power politics. He had secured his position as king over Palestine by manipulating Marcus Antonius. Fearful of plots to overthrow him, he also murdered several members of his own family (Mounce 1998:12). It would be normal for him to be suspicious of a new 'king of the Jews'. Herod did not want rivals and so he decided to kill the newborn Jewish 'king'.

Besides the political context for Jesus' escape to Egypt there is a religious dimension. In verse 15 Matthew tells us that the flight to Egypt fulfilled an Old Testament prophecy: 'This was to fulfil what had been spoken by the Lord through the prophet, 'Out of Egypt I called my son.'' The Old Testament quotation is taken from the book of Hosea chapter 11. This verse, in its original context, undoubtedly refers to the people of Israel (Davies & Allison 2000:263). Blomberg (1992:67) emphasises the fact that it is not a predictive prophecy but a recalling of God's love for Israel at the time of her exodus from Egypt. Blomberg draws attention to the spiritual aspect of both Israel's exodus and the arrival of the Messiah when he writes: 'Just as God brought the nation of Israel out of Egypt to inaugurate his original covenant with them, so again God is bringing the Messiah, who fulfils the hopes of Israel, out of Egypt as he is about to inaugurate his new covenant (:67)'. The same view is expressed by Luz (1989:146) when he writes that Israel's exodus from Egypt is repeated and completed in Jesus. Luz continues: 'The catchword "Egypt" is thus for Matthew just as decisive as the catchword "Son". This is the Matthean thought: salvation happens once more anew.'

With the story of Jesus' escape to Egypt and the quotation of Hos. 11:1

Matthew aligns Jesus and his family with Israel and her refugee experience (Senior 1998:47). Jesus, the son of God, has to leave his birthplace. He flees from persecution. But even when his persecutor is dead, the danger is still there. Jesus' family returns from Egypt, but they cannot stay in Judea. They have to move on to Nazareth in Galilee. Byrne (2004:31) comments: 'The family of Jesus have to yield before the naked force of worldly power. Like refugees today, they have no control over where they may safely live but face constant uprooting as circumstances determined by those in power change.' According to Schweizer (1976:42) Matthew gives geographical data to stress the fact that Jesus' life 'is destined to be a life of homeless wandering'. A confirming passage in Matthew's gospel stresses the fact that Jesus' followers will be wanderers just like him (cf. Gnilka 1986:311). In chap. 8 v. 20 Jesus speaks the following words to a scribe who wants to become one of his disciples: 'Foxes have holes, and birds of the air have nests; but the Son of Man has nowhere to lay his head.' In other words, Jesus does not have a place where he can sleep. He does not have what many people would consider basic - a place where one can rest (Morris 1995:200-201). He is 'devoid of all middle-class security' (Schweizer 1976:219). He is homeless on earth and anyone who follows him will experience the same homelessness (Mounce 1998:77).

## Jesus' followers

The New Testament authors provide us with various examples of followers of Jesus who went through the similar experiences of persecution and homelessness. In Acts 8:1, for example, Luke tells us that a severe persecution broke out in Jerusalem after Stephen's death and caused many believers to leave the city (:1). They first fled to Judea and Samaria (:1) but later also 'travelled as far as Phoenicia, Cyprus and Antioch' (11:19). This persecution, however, was a blessing in disguise, as these Christians 'who had been scattered preached the word wherever they went' (:4). As a result 'a great number of people believed and turned to the Lord' (11:21). In other words, Christian refugees became agents of God's mission. The same was true for Priscilla and Aquila, a refugee couple from Italy (Acts 18:2), who joined Paul's multicultural mission team in Corinth and accompanied him to Ephesus where they ministered to the new believers (:19). They later returned to Rome (cf. Rom. 16:3).

However, the most prominent example of a homeless and persecuted follower of Jesus and migratory agent of God's mission is the apostle Paul himself. Following his conversion the apostle spent some time in Arabia and Syria (Gal. 1:16-18). His first missionary journey led him to Cyprus (Acts 13:4), Perga (:13), Antioch of Pisidia (:14), Iconium (14:1), Lystra (:8), Derbe (:20), and Jerusalem (15:4). Other places he visited during his later journeys included Troas (16:8), Neapolis (:11), Philippi (:12), Thessalonica (Acts 17:1), Berea (:10), and Athens (:16). In some of these places Paul met with fierce opposition: in Lystra he was stoned (14:19), in Philippi severely flogged and imprisoned (16:23), and in Iconium both Jews and Gentiles plotted against him (14:5). All this, however, did not stop him. Paul's ambition was 'to preach the gospel where Christ was not known' (Rom. 15:20).

As a result of Paul's ministry both indigenous people and immigrants came to faith in Christ. Two examples of migrants who became Christians through the apostle's preaching can be found in Acts chapter 16. Thus, the name of Lydia, the first convert in Philippi (Acts 16:13-15), corresponds to the name of her birth place: She 'was an immigrant from Thyatira, a city in Lydia which was part of the Roman province of Asia Minor' (Prill 2008:72). The jailor, who is mentioned later in the same chapter (:29-34), was part of the Roman administration and doubtless a Roman himself (Matson 1996:156). Consequently, migrants were not only agents but also recipients of the mission of God and His Church.

# The treatment of foreigners in the Bible

## Foreigners in the Old Testament

In the Old Testament a foreigner who lived permanently among the Israelites is called a *ger*, which is often translated as *sojourner, resident alien,* or simply as *stranger* (Willis 1993:20). The same term is also used for Israelites living in a foreign territory. Spencer (1992:103) notes:

> In the biblical texts the term *gēr* is used in two basic ways: to describe the experiences of the Israelites themselves when they are living among foreigners; and to describe those non-Israelites who live among the Israelites. However, this distinction becomes confused when the claim is made that the Levites are *gērîm* (sojourners) among the Israelites. In all these cases, there are certain expectations of both the native population and the sojourners.

According to Collins (1994:840) sojourners or resident aliens formed a class within the Israelite community that descended from the old Canaanite population, from foreign servants and prisoners of war and from refugees, as well as other immigrants who wanted a new place in which they could live. Kellermann (1973:984) and Zehnder (2005:280) mention three main reasons for the forced migration of *gerim*: famine, war, and the fear of being taken into debt-slavery. The group of voluntary migrants among the *gerim*, writes Zehnder, consisted mostly of merchants, craftsmen, mercenaries, or agricultural workers (:280). However, the popular view that *gerim* were descendents of the Canaanite population is rejected by some authors (:281). Thus, in his commentary on Leviticus Noth (1965:131) writes that the *gerim* mentioned in 17:8-9 consisted both of Israelites and non-Israelites: 'Besides this, vv8-9 expressly place alongside the settled population the group of 'strangers', i.e. the group of those, whether Israelites or non-Israelites, who lived without any stake in the land among the settled population.' Bultmann (1992) goes even a step further. He argues that in the oldest Deuteronomic laws the term *ger* does not describe people of foreign origin but underprivileged Israelites, who similar to widows and orphans, lack the solidarity usually practised by the kinship group (:43-44).

The other category of alien residents is the *toshav* or *ger toshav* (Zehnder 2005:282). Some scholars believe that these immigrants were in no way distinctive from the *gerim*, while others claim that they were less integrated into the social and religious life of Israel (Zehnder 2005:283). Spencer (2004:88), for example, notes that in Leviticus and Numbers the term is used to describe social outsiders.

Finally, there is the group of *nokrim*, who are different from resident aliens (Zehnder 2005:283). These were foreigners who lived only temporarily among the Israelites, had no desire to assimilate into Israelite society, and enjoyed no special legal protection (:283). Konkel (1997a:109) writes that they were 'usually perceived as dangerous and hostile' and Spencer (2004:94) speaks of a less hospitable attitude towards them. This view is rejected by Bultmann (1992:102), who argues that there is no proof from the Deuteronomic law that the *nokrim* were seen as a threat. However, there is a good reason for the lack of special treatment: in the eyes of the law-giver the economic situation of these foreigners did not require any special support measures or protective legislation (Zehnder 2005:370). Bultmann (1992:102) mentions that economic independence was one of the main features of the *nokrim*.

One of the main characteristics of resident aliens was their landless status (cf. Bultmann 1992:55; Konkel 1997b:837; Rendtorff 2002:79; Wright 2004:94). Konkel (1997b:837) notes: 'The sojourner does not possess land and is generally in the service of an Israelite who is his master and protector (Deut 24:14).' Wright (2004:94) points out that they were completely dependent upon employment by land-owning Israelite households: 'As long as the host household retained its land and was economically viable, the position of these dependents was secure. But without such protection they were very vulnerable indeed.' Resident aliens who lacked the protection of a land-owning family were in a similar position to many widows or orphans, who had to rely on acts of charity (Wright 1990:103).

According to Exod. 23:12 and Deut. 5:14, resident aliens in Israel enjoyed equal status with the Israelites in observing the Sabbath rest (Rowell 2000:1235). Deut. 16:11&14 mention that they were to be included in the festival of weeks and the festival of booths. Konkel (1997b:837) claims that the participation in these feasts 'assumes the acceptance of circumcision', but Zehnder (2005:364) argues that the participation in these festivals was more of a formal nature. They were not expected to worship the God of Israel. Furthermore, resident aliens were entitled to fair treatment and legal protection (Rowell 2000:1235). In Deuteronomy 24:17 we find the following commandment: 'You shall not deprive a resident alien or an orphan of justice.' This command reminds the Israelites to treat the legal cases of the poor people with equal care as those of the rich and powerful members of society (Wright 1998:260). Other divine commands forbade the mistreatment or oppression of foreigners (Exod. 22:21, 32:9) or their economic exploitation (Deut. 24:14-15). Instead, the Israelites were called to love the strangers living among them and to treat them as citizens (Deut. 10:19, Lev. 19:25). Rivera-Pagán (2012:580) comments that '[c]aring for the stranger became a key element of the Torah, the covenant of justice and righteousness between Yahweh and Israel'.

There are two reasons given why Israel should treat foreigners in such a way. Firstly, Israel knew from firsthand experience what it was like to live as strangers in a foreign country. They had experienced oppression and persecution in Egypt for a long time. And so some of the commands explicitly remind Israel of this (Deut. 10:19, Deut. 24:14-17, Exod. 22:21, Lev. 19:25). Secondly, they are told that God loves foreigners, and therefore he expects them to do the same (Deut. 10:18). Weinfeld (1991:439) notes: 'God does not show particularity in judgment and does not discriminate between the rich and the poor, the residents and the alien (cf. 1:16-17, also 2 Chr 19:7). Men should therefore imitate God and love the alien too (v19).' This love command comes without any condition of assimilation (Zehnder 2005:344). Furthermore, the biblical authors make clear that the land the Israelites inhabit does not really belong to them. They have to regard themselves as foreigners living on God's land: 'The land shall not be sold in perpetuity, for the land is mine; with me you are but aliens and tenants' (Lev. 25:23). The Israelites are 'permanent but non-property owning [,] residents' (Porter 1976:201). In other words, they are in the same position as the resident aliens and foreigners who live among them (Rendtorff 2002:79). This idea of being strangers on God's land can also be found in 1 Chronicles 29:15 and Psalm 39:12.

In sum, one can say that according to the Old Testament law codes resident aliens had a special position in Israelite society. They were granted 'rights of assistance, protection, and religious participation' (Konkel 1997b:837). Zehnder (2005:401) comes to the conclusion that the relationship between Israelites and resident aliens/foreigners was not characterised by any form of racial or ethnic discrimination. Similarly Van Engen (2010:31) who notes: 'God does not only require that the stranger who lives in the midst of the People of Israel be treated fairly and equitably, but God also commands that the immigrant / stranger is to receive the care and compassion of the People of God.' However, Spencer (1992:104) argues that resident aliens did not enjoy the same status in society as the Israelites, even though equal treatment for them was the norm. For Spencer, the fact that the resident aliens are singled out in the Old Testament legislation is proof enough that they were not full members of society but people of different and lower status.

## Foreigners in the New Testament

One of the New Testament key passages describing the treatment of foreigners can be found in the parable of the sheep and the goats, which is told in Matt. 25:31-46. The parable points to the final separation of the righteous, who will inherit the kingdom of God, and those who will be deprived of this inheritance. The reason given for God's blessing of the righteous is their merciful response to other people's needs (Mounce 1998:236). Commentators differ in their interpretation of the term 'all the nations' (cf. Davies & Allison 2000:422). Stanton (1993:214), for example, favours the particularist interpretation of the phrase. He believes that Matthew is writing about all non-Christians. He finds the proof for this view in Matt. 24:30 which speaks of 'all the tribes of the earth' who will mourn at the coming of the Son of Man. Other scholars, such as Furnish (1972:80), hold that Matthew had all Christians in mind when he wrote about 'all the nations' that will be gathered before the throne of God. But the majority of scholars, it seems, interpret the judgment pictured in Matt. 25:31-46 as the final judgment of all humanity (cf. Beare 1981:493; Davies & Allison 2000:422; France 1999:354; Gaechter 1963:813; Gnilka 1988:371; Gundry 1982:511; Luz 2005:208; Nolland 2005:1024; Schlatter 1995:373-374; Schnackenburg

2002:256, Weber 1997:676). Byrne (2004:196), for example, writes that the particularist interpretation implies a separate judgment for Christians and non-Christians, which runs counter to the announcement in Matt. 16:27.

Altogether, Matthew mentions six different situations of need. One directly refers to the treatment of strangers: 'I was a stranger and you welcomed me' (25:35). Nolland (2005:1030) in his commentary on Matthew points to the similarity between hospitality-to-strangers and Jesus' command to love one's enemies. He writes: 'The welcoming of strangers, while not radical in the same way, has a family likeness to love of enemies in Mt. 5:43-48: both cases transcend focussing on one's self' (:1030). The Greek word for stranger, which Matthew uses here, is *xenos*. Bietenhard (1975:686) points out that the Greeks used *xenos* for people who did not belong to their own community. Bietenhard adds that in Greek society 'it was a sign of barbarity, when strangers were treated as if they had no rights and people did with them what they pleased' (:687). According to Morris (1995:638) *xenos* can even mean people who are exiled from their own countries. The passage emphasises the importance of caring for foreigners who have left their own countries, for whatever reason, and who need some kind of accommodation. Jesus identifies himself with such people, and anyone who practices hospitality towards them serves him (Matt. 25:38-40).

Scholars differ in their interpretation of the phrase 'these brothers of mine' in verse 40. Some argue that it refers to anyone in need (cf. Beare 1981:495; Davies & Allison 1997:429; Hill 1972:331; Schweizer 1995:159); others limit it to Jesus' disciples, i.e. to all Christians (France 1999:357; Overman 1996:349) or to Christian leaders and missionaries (Davies 1993:174; Gundry 1982:514; Luz 1996:129; Suh 2006:228). The context allows for multiple interpretation (cf. Heil 1998:14). Harrington (1991:357) points out that in several Matthean texts the phrase seems to describe Christians. According to Nolland (2005:1031-1032) this is also the case in 25:40:

> Jesus has those who are literally his brothers and sisters in 12:46-47; 13:55. But more important is the fictive family created by Jesus' identification in 12:48-50 of those who do the will of his Father as his brothers and sisters (and mother); in this sense the phrase will appear again in 28:10. For Matthew the same sort of identification seems to be involved in 25:40 (and

this implies that for him 'these' must relate to the group on the right).

Consequently, judgement is on the basis on people's response to Christians in need (Stanton 1993:227). For France (1999:355) this interpretation of verse 40 is much more in tune with the theological emphases of Matthew's Gospel as a whole. The purpose of Matthew 25:31-46, then, is to encourage Christian believers who face severe persecution and oppression (Stanton 1993:223). However, other scholars argue that the phrase 'these brothers of mine' is quite unique (cf. Gnilka 1988:375; Meier 1990:304). Schnackenburg (2002:258) writes that 'against the horizon of world judgment' it can be expanded to all people whether Christian or not. He goes to say:

> To understand only Christians or Christian missionaries as among the "least", on the ground of places in which "little ones" refers to disciples of Jesus, Christian missionaries, or insignificant members of the community..., is to overlook the fact that "in the name of a disciple" (10:42) is absent here (:258).

In other words, the stranger might be anyone, and not just some other Christian brother or sister.

Another important New Testament passage is Galatians 3:27-28. Here the apostle Paul stresses that Christian believers not only belong to God through faith in Christ but also to one another. They belong to each other in such a way that traditional distinctions which divide humankind become less important (Cole 1993:155-156). Paul writes in verse 28: 'There is neither Jew nor Greek, slave nor free, male nor female, for you are all one in Christ Jesus'. In other words, in God's Church there are no privileges because of one's racial or ethnic background, gender, education or social status. When the apostle wrote his letter to the Galatians the Greek perspective of the world was a world divided between Greeks and barbarians, whereas the Jews viewed the world as divided between Jews and Gentiles (Dunn 1993:205). People might have been brought up in different countries and cultures, some of them might be wealthy, others poor; but for believers in Christ these distinctions, though they undoubtedly exist, are not a bar to Christian fellowship.

According to Chester (1997:113) Paul's statement underlines that 'it is central to Paul's vision that the Christian community should be characterised by unity, equality and the breaking down of all barriers between its members.' Martyn 1998:381-383) speaks of a 'community of the new creation' in which unity in Christ has replaced any ethnic or religious distinctions on which the old creation was built upon. Put differently, Paul stresses that Christians have a new identity. They might be Jewish, Greek or Roman, but first and foremost they are children of God, whose true citizenship is in heaven (Phil. 3:20). They are united by their faith in Christ. This bond of unity has priority over any national, cultural or social allegiance. However, this oneness in Christ must be understood 'not as levelling and abolishing of all racial, social and gender differences, but as an integration of just said differences into a common participation 'in Christ', wherein they enhance...the unity of the body, and enrich the mutual interdependence and service of its members' (Dunn 1993:208).

It should not surprise us that Paul's views on race and ethnicity can also be found in the teachings of Jesus. When Jesus was confronted with the question 'And who is my neighbour?' he responded by telling the story of the *Good Samaritan* (Luke 10:25-37). Many scholars argue that the questioner, a Jewish lawyer, was struggling with the idea that neighbourly love should go beyond national and ethnic boundaries (cf. Morris 1994:206; Evans 2002:176; Bock 2008:1028). As an expert in the law, the man was certainly aware of Old Testament passages, such as Leviticus 19:33-34 and Micah 6:8 (cf. Wiersbe 2003:16). He knew what was required of him: 'to show mercy, even to strangers and enemies' (:116). He was 'challenged by God's demand' (Bock 2008:1028) but his prejudice was too strong. He wanted 'to draw boundary lines' (Jones 1999:106) and 'to quiet his conscience' (Hendriksen 1984:593). Keith Ferdinando (2008:62), who seems to agree with this popular interpretation of Jesus' parable, (2008:62) comments:

> [T]he story of the Samaritan...confronts and subverts the particular ethnic prejudice of Jesus' own hearers. Its message is so easily reduced to banality today, but in its context it was 'radical and upsetting' and was doubtless heard in stunned silence as it challenged – almost scandalously so – the deepest assumptions of the original audience. It continues to demand a fun-

damental change of values, a seismic transformation of attitude and act: 'loving one's neighbour is to transcend all racial and cultural boundaries'.

However, as Legg (2011:24) argues the Jewish scribe was probably also aware of the use of the word *neighbour* in Leviticus 19:17-18. Here neighbour is understood as one's 'brother' and 'one of your people'. Therefore, it is very likely that the Jewish lawyer believed that only a Jewish fellow-believer could be a neighbour, i.e. a member of the covenant people of God. Marshall (1978:450) seems to support this interpretation when he writes: 'Jewish usage excluded Samaritans and foreigners from this category.' Consequently, the main point of Jesus' parable is not so much an appeal to show compassion to people in need regardless of their ethnic or racial background as many scholars suggest (e.g. Geldenhuys 1988:311; Jones 1999:107; Bock 2008:1035; Evens 2002:176-177) but a much more radical claim: membership in God's Church crosses national boundaries. Legg (2011:27-28) writes:

> Where the priest and the Levite fail, the third man passes the test. But the man is not an Israelite at all; he is a Samaritan. Jesus is teaching that the Samaritan is the one who behaves as a true Israelite should! He is the one who treats the injured man as a neighbour should. 'Who was a neighbour to the man who fell into the hands of the robbers?' asks Jesus. The answer is, 'The Samaritan', even though the Jewish listener would not soil his lips with the name. The real shock of the parable is only felt when, and if, the Jewish listeners hear Jesus saying that a Samaritan is behaving as, and therefore is, a true Israelite, a neighbour of all other Israelites, a covenant-keeper. The priest and the Levite, on the other hand, behave unlike neighbours and therefore are not neighbours. Jesus has, in effect, admitted a Samaritan to membership of the covenant people and excommunicated the priest and the Levite – and anyone who lives and behaves like them – from the people of God.

# Conclusion

Maruskin (2000:197) writes that the 'Bible is the ultimate immigration handbook, a book written by, for, and about immigrants and refugees'. While the term 'immigration handbook' appears to be an overstatement, the examples above indicate that the Bible gives emphasis to people who were forced to leave their homes and live abroad. Migration is, as Rivera-Pagán (2012:588) states 'fundamental to the biblical narratives'. The Bible cites many examples of people who migrated to other countries in order to survive. They had to flee from political or religious persecution, economic exploitation or natural catastrophes. Many Africans can identify with the biblical accounts. Displacements by famine or civil unrest are a common experience in Africa. The experience of being a stranger is well known. Often it is women who suffer most. Isabel Apawo Phiri (2006:320) comments: 'Being a refugee is a stressful experience for anyone, but it is particularly difficult for women and girls because it can lead to sexual abuse and the spread of HIV/AIDS.'

The biblical narrative, however, is explicit and prescriptive when dealing with migration and its effects. It makes clear that God has a special concern for foreigners and ethnic minorities. He loves them and wants them to be treated with respect. It also makes clear that migrants of different cultural and ethnic backgrounds are agents of God's mission to bless all nations on earth by introducing them to Christ and his gospel of salvation. Last but not least, the Bible points to migrants who find faith in the living God through the ministry of indigenous Christians and other migrants.

In addition, the New Testament writings emphasize that Christians, whatever their ethno-cultural background, have a new identity. They are united through their common faith in Christ. This principle of unity calls Christians to integrate migrants, foreigners and members of national minority groups into multi-ethnic churches.

In sum, the picture which the Bible paints of the Church is that of a multicultural and multi-ethnic pilgrim community, a community of foreigners, migrants and ambassadors 'whose land and nation are not of this earth' (Girgis 2010:43).

Consequently, Christians should welcome strangers and migrants – in southern Africa and elsewhere. Celestin Musekura (2006:321), a Rwandan theologian, explains what such a welcome might look like with regard to forced migrants:

> Not only should we minister to refugees' spiritual and pastoral needs, but they should be encouraged to minister to us by sharing in our worship, fellowship, service and ministries. Their insights can enrich our own Christian experience and they can become missionaries in our communities, just as the early Christians did in similar circumstances (Acts 8:1-4; 18:1-2). Such recognition will start to restore their dignity and hope (:321).

*This research paper is partly based on Thorsten Prill's DTh thesis from the University of South Africa published under the title 'Global Mission on our Doorstep: Forced Migration and the Future of the Church'(Münster: MV Wissenschaft, 2008).*

# Bibliography

Albright, WF & Mann, CS 1971. Matthew: introduction, translation and notes. New York: Doubleday.

Amos, C 2004. The book of Genesis. Peterborough: Epworth Press.

Ashby, G 1998. Go out and meet God: a commentary on the book of Exodus. Grand Rapids: Eerdmans.

Atkinson, D 1999. The message of Ruth. Leicester: Inter-Varsity Press.

Ballard, R 2002. Race, ethnicity and culture. First published in: New directions in sociology, M Holborn (ed). Ormskirk: Causeway.

Beare, FW 1981. The gospel according to Matthew: a commentary. Oxford: Basil Blackwell.

Berlin, A 2005. Psalms and the literature of exile: psalms 137, 44, 69 and 78, in The book of psalms: commentary and reception, PW Flint & PD Miller (eds). Leiden: Brill.

Bietenhard, H 1975. Xenos, in The new international dictionary of New Testament theology, Vol. 1, C Brown (ed). Exeter: Paternoster Press, 686-690.

Blomberg, CL 1992. Matthew: a commentary. Nashville: Broadman Press.

Blume, MA 2000. Refugees and mission: a primer. Mission Studies 17(1/2):162-172.

Bock, DIL 2008. Luke 9:51-24:53. Grand Rapids: Baker Academic

Broyles, CC 1999. Psalms. Peabody: Hendrickson.

Brueggemann, W 1982. Genesis. Atlanta: John Knox Press.

Bultmann, C 1992. Der Fremde im antiken Juda: Eine Untersuchung zum sozialen Typenbegriff ›ger‹ und seinem Bedeutungswandel in der alttestamentlichen Gesetzgebung. Göttingen: Vandenhoeck & Ruprecht.

Bush, F 1996. Word biblical commentary: Ruth/Esther. Nashville: Thomas Nelson Publisher.

Byrne, B 2004. Lifting the burden: reading Matthew's gospel in the church today. Collegeville: The Liturgical Press.

Campbell, EF 1993. The book of Ruth, in The Oxford companion to the bible, BM Metzger & MD Coogan (eds). New York: Oxford University Press, 662-664.

Chama, E 2010. Tribalism killing dream for African church. The Southern Cross. <http://www.scross.co.za/2010/10/tribalism-killing-dream-for-african-church/>

Chester, A 1997. The Pauline communities, in A vision for the church, M Bockmuehl & MB Thompson (eds). Edinburgh: T&T Clark, 105-120.

Childs, BS 1974. Exodus: a commentary. London: SCM Press.

Clements, RE 1972. Exodus. Cambridge: Cambridge University Press.

Coggins, R 2000. The book of exodus. Peterborough: Epworth Press.

Cole, RA 1985. Exodus: an introduction and commentary. London: The Tyndale Press.

Cole, RA 1993. Galatians. Leicester: Inter-Varsity Press.

Collins, AO 1994. Sojourner/resident alien, in Lutterworth dictionary of the Bible, WE Mills (gen ed). Cambridge: Lutterworth Press, 840.

Cosgrove, CH 2006. Did Paul value ethnicity?. Catholic Biblical Quarterly 68(2):268-290.

Cotter, DW 2003. Exodus. Collegeville: The Liturgical Press.

Coxon, PW 1989. Was Naomi a scold? A response to Fewell and Gunn. Journal for the Study of the Old Testament 45:25-37.

Craghan, J 1982. Esther, Judith, Tobit, Jonah, Ruth. Wilmington: Michael Glazier.

Davies, GH 1973. Exodus. London: SCM Press.

Davies, M 1993. Matthew. Sheffield: JSOT Press.

Davies, WD & Allison, DC 1997. The Gospel according to Saint Matthew, Vol.3. Edinburgh: T&T Clark.

Davies, WD & Allison, DC 2000. The Gospel according to Saint Matthew, Vol.1. Edinburgh: T&T Clark.

Dummett, M 2001. On immigration and refugees. London: Routledge.

Dunn, JDG 1993. Commentary on the epistle to the Galatians. London: A&C Black.

Durham, JI 1987. Word biblical commentary: Exodus. Waco: Word Books.

Eaton, M 2000. Preaching through the Bible: Judges and Ruth. Tonbridge: Sovereign World.

Evans, CA 2002. Luke. Peabody: Hendrickson.

Fenton, S 2003. Ethnicity. Cambridge: Polity.

Ferdinando, K 2008. The ethnic enemy- no Greek nor Jew...Barbarian, Scythian: the gospel and ethnic difference. Themelios 33(2):48-63.

Fischer, I 2001. Rut. Freiburg: Herder.

France RT 1999. Matthew. Leicester: Inter-Varsity Press.

France, RT 2002. The Jewish dispersion, in The lion handbook to the bible, D Alexander & P Alexander (eds). Oxford: Lion Publishing, 753.

Fretheim, TE 1991. Exodus: a bible commentary for teaching and preaching. Louisville: John Knox Press.

Fuerst, WJ 1975. The books of Ruth, Esther, Ecclesiastes, the Song of Songs, Lamentations. Cambridge: Cambridge University Press.

Furnish, VP 1972. The love command of the New Testament. Nashville: Abingdon Press.

Gaechter, P 1963. Das Matthäus Evangelium. Innsbruck: Tyrolia Verlag.

Garrett, SR 1990. Exodus from bondage: Luke 9:31 and Acts 12:1-24. Catholic Biblical Quarterly 52(4):656-680.

Gathogo, JM 2007. Revisiting African hospitality in post-colonial Africa. Missionalia

35(2):108-130.

Gibson, JCL 1990. Genesis, Vol.2. Edinburgh: St. Andrew Press.

Girgis, R 2011. "House of prayer for all people": a biblical foundation for multicultural ministry. International Review of Mission 100(1):62-73.

Gnilka, J 1986. Das Matthäusevangelium I Teil. Freiburg: Herder.

Gnilka, J 1988. Das Matthäusevangelium II Teil. Freiburg: Herder.

Gundry, RH 1982. Matthew: a commentary on his literary and theological art. Grand Rapids: Eerdmans.

Hagedorn, AC 2007. Looking at foreigners in biblical and Greek prophecy. Vetus Testamentum 57:432-448.

Hagner, DA 1993. Word biblical commentary: Matthew 1-13. Dallas: Word Books.

Hamilton, VP 1990. The book of Genesis chapters 1-17. Grand Rapids: Eerdmans.

Hamlin, EJ 1996. A commentary on the book of Ruth. Edinburgh: The Handsel Press.

Hanciles, JJ 2003. Migration and mission: some implications for the twenty-first-century church. International Bulletin of Missionary Research 27(4):146-153.

Hanciles, JJ 2004. Beyond Christendom: African migration and transformations in global Christianity. Studies in World Christianity 10(1):93-113.

Harrington, DJ 1991. The Gospel of Matthew. Collegeville: The Liturgical Press.

Hawley, C 2008. Refugees flee South Africa attack. BBC news. <http://news.bbc.co.uk/2/hi/africa/7404351.stm>

Heil, JP 1998. The double meaning of the narrative of universal judgment in Matthew 25:31-46. Journal for the Study of the New Testament 69:3-14.

Henderiksen, W 1984. The gospel of Luke. Edinburgh: The Banner of Truth Trust.

Hiebert, D 2005. Ethnicity, in The dictionary of human geography, RJ Johnston, D Gregory, G Pratt & M Watts (eds). Oxford: Blackwell Publishing, 235-238.

Hill, D 1972. The Gospel of Matthew. London: Oliphants.

Hobbs, TR 1985. Word biblical commentary: 2 Kings. Waco: Word Books.

House, PR 1998. Old Testament theology. Downers Grove: Inter-Varsity Press.

Hubbard, RL 1988. The book of Ruth. Grand Rapids: Eerdmans.

Hudiburg, AH 2000. Famine, in Eerdmans dictionary of the bible, Freedman DN (ed). Grand Rapids: Eerdmans, 455-456.

Ihle, A 2009. Migration, integration and xenophobia in South Africa. München: Grin.

Jacques, A 1986. The stranger within your gates: uprooted people in the world today. Geneva: WCC Publications.

Jaeger, H 2003. Welcome the stranger. Christianity + Renewal December:34-37.

Janzen, JG 1993. Abraham and all the families of the earth: a commentary on the book of Genesis 12-50. Grand Rapids: Eerdmans.

Janzen, JG 1997. Exodus. Louisville: Westminster John Knox Press.

Jones, GH 1984. 1 and 2 Kings, Vol.2. London: Marshall, Morgan & Scott.

Jones, S 1999. Discovering Luke's gospel. Leicester: Crossway Books.

Kellermann, D 1993. Gûr, in Theologisches Wörterbuch zum Alten Testament, GJ Botterweck & H Ringgren (eds). Stuttgart: Kohlhammer, 979-991.

Kliot, N 2000. Global migration and ethnicity: contemporary case-studies, in Geographies of global change. RJ Johnston, PJ Taylor & MJ Watts (eds). Oxford: Blackwell, 175-190.

Klotz, A 2000. Migration after apartheid: deracialising South African foreign policy. Third World Quarterly 21(5):831-847.

Knight, GAF 1983. Psalms Vol.2. Louisville: Westminster John Knox Ppress.

Kok, P, Gelderblom, D, Ouch, JO & van Zyl, J 2006. Migration in South and Southern Africa: dynamics and determinants. Cape Town: HSRC Press.

Konkel, AH 1997a. 5797 nēkar, in New international dictionary of Old Testament theology & exegesis, Vol.3, WA VanGemeren (gen. ed). Carlisle: Paternoster Press, 108-109.

Konkel, AH 1997b. 1591 gwr, in New international dictionary of Old Testament theology & exegesis, Vol.1, WA VanGemeren (gen. ed). Carlisle: Paternoster Press, 836-839.

Köstenberger, AJ & O'Brien, PT 2001. Salvation to the ends of the earth: a biblical theology of mission. Leicester: IVP.

Kraus, H-J 1989. Psalms 60-150: a commentary, HC Oswald (trans.). Minneapolis: Augsburg Fortress.

Kümmel, WG 1995. Introduction to the New Testament. London: SCM.

Larkin, KJA 1996. Ruth and Esther. Sheffield: Sheffield Academic Press.

LaSor, WS, Hubbard, DA & Bush, FW 1982. Old Testament survey: the message, form and background of the Old Testament. Grand Rapids: Eerdmans.

Leech, K 2005. Changing society and the churches: race. London: SPCK.

Legg, J 2011. So who is my neighbour. Foundations: an international journal of evangelical theology 61(2):24-30.

Lincoln, A 2003. Ethnicity, in Oxford concise dictionary of politics. I McLean & A McMillan (eds). Oxford: Oxford University Press, 177-178.

Luz, U 1989. Mathew 1-7: a continental commentary, WC Linss (trans.). Minneapolis: Fortress Press.

Luz, U 1996. The theology of the Gospel of Matthew, JB Robinson (trans). Cambridge: Cambridge University Press.

Luz, U 2005. Studies in Matthew, R Selle (trans.). Grand Rapids: Eerdmans.

Lynch, JP & Simon, RJ 2003. Immigration the world over: statues, policies, and practicies. Lanham: Rowan & Littlefield.

Marshall, IH 1978. The gospel of Luke. Exeter: Paternoster

Marshall, IH 1999. The Acts of the Apostles. Leicester: Inter-Varsity Press.

Martin, RP 1997. Approaches to New Testament exegesis, in New Testament interpretation. IH Marshall (ed). Carlisle: Paternoster Press, 220-251.

Martyn JL 1988. Galatians: a new translation with introduction and commentary. New York: Doubleday.

Maruskin, J 2000, Ministering to the refugee Christ. Mission Studies 17(1/2):196-206.

Matson, DL 1996. Household conversion narratives in Acts: pattern and interpretation. Sheffield: Sheffield Academic Press.

Matthews, VH 2004. Judges and Ruth. Cambridge: Cambridge University Press.

Mc Laughlin, JL 2000. Elohim, in Eerdmans dictionary of the bible. DN Freedman (ed).Grand Rapids: Eerdmans.

Meier, JP 1990. Matthew. Collegeville: The Liturgical Press.

Meyers, C 2005. Exodus. Cambridge: Cambridge University Press.

Modi, R 2003. Migration to democratic South Africa. Economic and Political Weekly 38(18):1759-1762.

Moore, M 2000. Ruth, in Joshua, Judges, Ruth, J Harris, G Brown & M Moore (eds). Peabody: Hendrickson.

Morris, L 1994. Luke: an introduction and commentary. Leicester: Inter-Varsity Press.

Morris, L 1995. The Gospel according to Matthew. Leicester: Inter-Varsity Press.

Mounce, RH 1998. Matthew. Carlisle: Paternoster Press.

Musekura, C 2006. Refugees, in Africa Bible Commentary. Adeyemo, T (gen.ed.). Grand Rapids: Zondervan.

Nielsen, K 1997. Ruth: a commentary. Louisville: Westminster John Knox Press.

Nolland, J 2005. The Gospel of Matthew: a commentary on the Greek text. Grand Rapids: Eerdmans.

Noth, M 1962. Exodus, JS Bowden (trans). London: SCM Press.

Noth, M 1965. Leviticus, JE Anderson (trans). London: SCM Press.

Overman, JA 1996. Church and community: the Gospel according to Matthew. Valley Forge: Trinity Press International.

Oxford dictionaries. <http://oxforddictionaries.com/>

Payne, JD 2012. Strangers next door: immigration, migration, and mission. Downers Grove: IVP.

Pellerin, H 1998. Global restructuring and international migration: consequences for the globalization of politics, in Globalization: theory and practice, E Kofman & G Youngs (eds). London: Pinter, 81-96.

Phiri, IA 2006. Ruth, in Africa Bible Commentary. Adeyemo, T (gen. ed.). Grand Rapids: Zondervan.

Pohl, CD 2003. Biblical issues in mission and migration. Missiology: An International Review 31(1):3-15.

Pohl, CD 2006. Responding to strangers: insights from the Christian tradition. Studies in Christian Ethics 19(1):81-101.

Pohor, R 2006. Tribalism, ethnicity and race, in Africa Bible Commentary. Adeyemo, T (gen. ed.). Grand Rapids: Zondervan.

Porter, JR 1976. Leviticus. Cambridge: Cambridge University Press.

Prill, T 2005. Evangelism, theology and the church. Evangelical Review of Theology 29(4):309-330.

Prill, T 2008. Global mission on our doorstep: forced migration and the future of the church. Münster: MV Wissenschaft.

Prill, T 2009. Migration, mission and the multi-ethnic church. Evangelical Review of Theology 33(4):332-346.

Punt, J 2009. Post-apartheid racism in South Africa: the Bible, social identity and stereotyping. Religion & Theology16:246-272.

Ratcliffe, P 2004. Race, ethnicity and difference: imagining the inclusive society. Maidenhead: Open University Press.

Rendtorff, R 2002. The gēr in the priestly laws of the Pentateuch, in Ethnicity and the bible, MG Brett (ed). Leiden: Brill, 77-87.

Rex, J 1999. The nature of ethnicity in the project of migration, in The ethnicity reader, M Guibernau & J Rex (eds). Cambridge: Polity Press, 269-283.

Rex, J 2002, The fundamentals of the theory of ethnicity, in Making sense of collectivity: ethnicity, nationalism and globalisation, S Malesevic & M Haugaard (eds). London: Pluto Press, 88-121.

Rienecker, F 1984. Das Evangelium des Mätthaus. Wuppertal: R. Brockhaus.

Rivera-Pagán, NL 2012. Xenophilia or xenophobia: towards a theology of migration. Ecumenical Review 64(4):575-589.

Robinson, J 1976. The Second Book of Kings. Cambridge: Cambridge University Press.

Rogerson, JW & McKay, JW 1977. Psalms 101-150. Cambridge: Cambridge University Press.

Rowell, EL 2000. Sojourner, in Eerdmans dictionary of the bible, DN Freedman (ed). Grand Rapids: Eerdmans, 1235-1236.

Sakenfeld, KD 1999. Ruth. Louisville: John Knox Press.

Sarna, NM 1986. Exploring exodus: the origins of biblical Israel. New York: Schocken Books.

Sarna, NM 1991. The jps torah commentary: Exodus. Philadelphia: The Jewish Publication Society.

Sassen, S 1999. Guests and aliens. New York: The New Press.

Segatti, A 2011. Migration to South Africa: regional challenges versus national instruments and interests, in Contemporary migration to South Africa: a regional development issue. Segatti, A & LB Landau, LB (eds). Washington: The World Bank.

Schaefer, K 2001. Psalms. Collegeville: The Liturgical Press.

Schlatter A 1995. Das Evangelium nach Matthäus. Stuttgart: Calver Verlag.

Schnackenburg, R 2002. The Gospel of Matthew. Grand Rapids: Eerdmans.

Schweizer, E 1976. The good news according to Matthew, DE Green (trans). London: SPCK.

Schweizer, E 1995. Matthew's church, in The interpretation of Matthew. GN Stanton (ed). Edinburgh: T&T Clark, 149-177.

Senior, D 1998. Matthew. Nashville: Abingdon Press.

Sharp, J 2008. Fortress SA: xenophobic violence in South Africa. Anthropology Today 24(4):1-3.

Smith, MS 2007. "Your people shall be my people": family and covenant in Ruth 1:16-17. Catholic Biblical Quarterly 69(2):242-258.

Spencer, JR 1992. Sojourner, in The anchor bible dictionary, Vol.6, DN Freedman (ed). New York: Doubleday, 103-104.

Spencer, N 2004. Asylum and immigration: a Christian perspective on a polarised debate. Milton Keynes: Paternoster Press.

Stanton, GN 1993. A gospel for a new people: studies in Matthew. Louisville: Westminster/John Knox Press.

Stuhlmueller, C 2002. The spirituality of the psalms. Collegeville: The Liturgical Press.

Suh, JS 2006. Das Weltgericht und die Matthäische Gemeinde. Novum Testamentum 48(3):217-233.

Sztucki, J 1999. Who is a refugee? The convention definition: universal or obsolete? in Refugee rights and realities, F Nicholson & P Twomey (eds). Cambridge: Cambridge University Press, 55-80.

Tötemeyer, G 2010. Church and state in Namibia: the politics of reconciliation. Freiburg: Arnold-Bergstraesser-Institut.

Turner, LA 2000. Genesis. Sheffield: Sheffield Academic Press.

Van Engen, C 2010. Biblical perspectives on the role of immigrants in God's mission. Evangelical Review of Theology 34(1):29-43.

Van Seters, J 1994. The life of Moses: the Yahwist as historian in Exodus-Numbers. Louisville: Westminister/John Knox Press.

Walls, AF 2002a. Mission and migration: the diaspora factor in Christian history. Journal of African Christian Thought 5(2):3-11.

Walls, AF 2002b. The cross-cultural process in Christian history. Maryknoll: Orbis.

Weber, K 1997. The image of sheep and goats in Matthew 25:31-46. Catholic Biblical Quarterly 59(4):657-678.

Weinfeld, M 1991. Deuteronomy 1-11: a new translation with introduction and commentary. New York: Doubleday.

Wciser, A 1962. The Psalms: a commentary. London: SCM Press.

Wenham, GJ 1987. Word biblical commentary. Volume 1. Genesis 1-15. Waco: Word Books.

Westermann, C 1987. Genesis: a practical commentary. Grand Rapids: Eerdmans.

Wiersbe, WW 2003. Be compassionate: an expository study of Luke 1-13.Colorado Springs: Chariot Victor Publishing.

Willis, TM 1993. Alien, in The Oxford companion to the bible, BM Metzger & MD Coogan (eds). New York: Oxford University Press, 20.

Winn Leith, MJ 2001. Israel among the nations, in The Oxford history of the biblical world, MD Coogan (ed). Oxford: Oxford University Press, 276-316.

Wright, CJH 1990. God's people in God's land: family, land, and property in the Old Testament. Exeter: Paternoster Press.

Wright, CJH 1998. Deuteronomy. Peabody: Hendrickson.

Wright, CJH 2004. Old Testament ethics for the people of God. Downers Grove: Inter-Varsity Press.

Younger, KL 2002. Judges and Ruth. Grand Rapids: Zondervan.

Zehnder, M 2005. Umgang mit Fremden in Israel und Assyrien: Ein Beitrag zur Anthropologie des Fremden im Licht antiker Quellen. Stuttgart: Kohlhammer.

# Biographical notes

Thorsten Prill

*DTh (UNISA), MTh (OU), PgDipLRM (Sheffield), CThM (Nottingham), Dipl-Volksw. (Duisburg)*

Thorsten Prill is a Crosslinks mission partner lecturing in missiology, practical theology and systematic theology at Namibia Evangelical Theological Seminary (NETS). Before coming to Namibia he was pastor of two churches in the UK and Lutheran & International Chaplain at the University of Nottingham. He is the author of two books, *German Protestantism and the Spirit of God* (2010) and *Global Mission on our Doorstep* (2008). He has also edited several other books, including *Mission Namibia* (2012) and *God's Mission in Southern Africa* (2011). He has published articles in various journals, such as *Evangelical Review of Theology, Evangel, Foundations,* and *Evangelical Missions Quarterly.* Thorsten Prill serves as an Associate Pastor at Inner-City Lutheran Congregation, Windhoek.

**Namibia Evangelical Theological Seminary (NETS)**
PO Box 158
Windhoek
NAMIBIA

Email: tprill@nets.edu.na
Website: www.nets.edu.na

# YOUR KNOWLEDGE HAS VALUE

- We will publish your bachelor's and master's thesis, essays and papers

- Your own eBook and book - sold worldwide in all relevant shops

- Earn money with each sale

Upload your text at www.GRIN.com
and publish for free